T009460S

Country
Club

Country Club

Andy McGuire

Coach House Books, Toronto

first edition

Published with the generous assistance of the Canada Council for the Arts and the Ontario Arts Council. Coach House Books also acknowledges the support of the Government of Canada through the Canada Book Fund and the Government of Ontario through the Ontario Book Publishing Tax Credit.

LIBRARY AND ARCHIVES CANADA CATALOGUING IN PUBLICATION
McGuire, Andy, 1983-, author
     Country club / Andy McGuire.

Poems.
Issued in print and electronic formats.
ISBN 978-1-55245-320-9 (paperback).

     I. Title.

PS8625.G845C68 2015   C811'.6   C2015-905042-1

Country Club is available as an ebook: ISBN 978 1 77056 422 0

Purchase of the print version of this book entitles you to a free digital copy. To claim your ebook of this title, please email sales@chbooks.com with proof of purchase or visit chbooks.com/digital. (Coach House Books reserves the right to terminate the free digital download offer at any time.)

CONTENTS

POOL

I'm too tired to care today.
It costs too much to care what you say.
I love you too much to care anyway.
I write *I love you too much to care* on my resumé.
I hear they're hiring masseuses at the New York City Ballet.
I left my car with the man from Bombay
They pay

To play
The man from Bombay
Who bobbles through the dossier
Of things George Washington would have him say.
Beautivul day.
Right avay.
Selective hearing will forever outweigh

The fact that the past is here to stay.
Throw a stone and you get three cheers for the NRA.
Everyone under the sun is killing a power play.
A wedding is underway.
They vow each word like vertebrae.
The bride has died and gone to heaven, and I catch the bouquet.
It must be my birthday.

Eat, pray
And stay the fuck away
From my cabana. I wave the waiter over and order an El Presidente
Then brush him off, *Ándale!*
Carry on with your *beaux idées*,
At sunrise the horse's mouth hits the hay.
Eat, pray

And delete your browsing history. Whatever you think you saw is hearsay.
I care in a cowboy-wrangling-a-stray
Kind of way.
I throw what I say
An exclusive soiree
And pull out my impression of JFK
In which I lay

Low, having a bad hair day,
Bleeding, all blasé.
Not bleeding per se –
Bleeding is not my forte,
Comprende?
Rome was built on a day like today.
Namaste.

HAPPY HOUR

Clementines are sweeter going ninety,
Flip-booking by, pink flamingos,
Christmas south of the Mason–Dixon,
Alabama synonymous with *awesome*,
Signs jonesing for Jesus
Upping the ante as our avatar nosedives
Latitude lines on the GPS,
Caught on a wave of leaving.
Ontario will never have Florida oranges
And blues. We winter with impunity
In the womb of the Coupon State,
Where one can spend a lifetime trying to say
Something dazzling about the Gulf,
Hailing daily incompletions like an eagle
Dropping dry hearts on the one-yard line.

BLACK BOX

Black blood spots a field of snow.
I race to write this down,
Black blood spotting
The snow as I go.

Call and I come
Bounding back with a rabbit.
I can't help myself.
Submission is such an embarrassing habit.

Already dead in dog years,
I call and the future comes faster
Than a flock of fallen ducks.
Slavishly licking the wound of hunger,

Offal and all,
I suck the bones of Best in Show.
The connection I sense
Between bladder and plough

Is enough to tell
The tail between my legs is yours.
Call and I come
Like a mutt depositing yellow.

Where he goes, I go.
The snow is all but drinkable.
I am down on all fours
To do the unthinkable.

DOLPHIN

The air wears the scent
Of coconut and sautéing skin.
I skim the deep end
On a blow-up dolphin.

A bikini speaks to me,
My imagination takes a vacation.
I look and then I look some more.
Looking is the local currency,

Looking is what bikinis are for.
She reaches for lotion.
My dolphin squirms
At all the commotion.

The money shot is coming.
The money shot shouts, *Coming!*
The money shot shot the sheriff
Over tanning tariffs.

The rich get richer and so they should.
My money is good
As gone with a taste for top-notch.
A waitress watches me watch.

CANADIAN WATER

A centrefold impaled on a birch branch
Is where freewheeling moose
And the painter and his canoe collide
With subpar ollies, summer day jobs
And the bones of bush parties,

When every channel still has a helicopter
And the lost mothers of department stores
Desperately comb through thickets of clothes.
Every tree in the country has a painting to its name.
Graffiti goes against the grain.

Left of *Slayer*, below *fuck love* and *Brian is a homo*,
A Sharpie heart frames a pair of initials
Long after the backseat of the beater of their bloom.
A familiar face I almost met too many times to remember
Hauled all of the picnic tables into the trees.

I love this place enough to deface
With a lavender portrait of her,
Acrylic crows overseeing the landing
Where I disembark
And lick the icing off Tom Thomsons,

Splinters turning to branches bearing fruit in the shape of my face.
Here comes the hot pink dawn rising over the horses
Of a drunk, a sasquatch, an amateur arsonist,
As the dream drips on,
Breathing down the neck of the archivist.

MINOR KINGDOMS

Drifting with my Daisy
One lazy afternoon,
The world was a fall fair
Where you shoot balloons.
I took aim.
The bird epilepsied from the rafters,
Left eye socket usurped
By a silver pellet.
To see it suffer was not
What I was after.
It was embarrassing.
I cocked and shot
Until my Daisy shook.
I lost count of the shots it took.

WINDOW

The same man drives by a dozen times a day.
His first pass is morning coffee.
After the second I have a day on my hands.
Leading theories for the third include secret smoker,
Vehicular pride and scratch cards.
The fourth dated a department store model in the nineties.
Five doesn't come with instructions.
Six's long-lost roommate never got over the traffic-cone incident.
Seven drinks its weight in gin and weighs in
On the Batman/Superman debate.
Trying to reason with eight is like medicating the dead.
Hallmark conducts market research on the occasion of the ninth.
Ten finally let Jesus and scrapbooking into its life.
Don't look eleven in the eye
Unless you want to wake with a myoclonic jerk on an airplane.
Twelve is a man driving by a window, wondering
Why that guy just sits there all day.

MUSIC ROW

I refuse to pay for a shot
I thought was on the house.
A man the size of a rhino appears
And escorts me to a room

With a drip painting of blood for a floor.
This has all been done before.
He calls it *theft of services*
In speech that sounds rehearsed.

None of this was in the Nashville brochure.
Locked in a staring contest with freedom,
I count his freckles out loud,
His nose a mountain covered in tulips.

I try for a photo
But he does an about-face.
It never pans out when I go to hug a ghost.
Hard to have a final say

When the thousand words that got away
Could be anywhere by now.
This always happens
When I buy a fish a river.

A soundproof room
Where no cell signal can follow.
The problem never gets old.
I'm told the only way out is through the tulips.

INTELLIGENT LIFE

Breakfast is battleground.
Eggs, grenades.

You make love like a horse
On the Parthenon.

Fuck you and the you you rode in on.
Our house on a hill

Burns at both ends,
Empty rooms prescriptions

We refuse to fill.
I wish you would

Misunderstand me
The way you used to

Before you found out
About emotional branding

And the red right hand
Of the last statue standing.

ZERO EXPERIENCE

The Agency tells us the world is our oyster.
They say optimism is an art,
The slice of the pie chart that remains cheerful
Through starving. Temping is all about potential.

You can't stop a fire that doesn't start.
All my matches were made in China.
I've hit my head too many times
Dancing in the dark. The odd Friday afternoon

Francine serenades our frayed platoon
In the crude theatre we call the copy room.
She has a history of using colourful language
In the workplace. Being let go is a refrain.

I daydream of her doorbell
But a gulf of grey separates her cubicle from mine.
Too many people are sitting in this oyster.
Management will have to put up a sign.

MICHELANGELO IN REVERSE

She wanted to draw me.
Draw was code.
Over she came and off came the clothes.
She drew me all night

In every possible pose.
Art is a horse with a Teflon saddle.
The art part stays on top
Of the bucking.

Her drawing started sucking.
Art is hard.
Art doesn't give a damn,
Art won't send a St. Bernard.

She straddles the smokestack
Overseeing my remains.
Black is the new black.
Once you go black

You never get back in the saddle.
She blows my brains
Into bubblegum sunsets
And signs the back in ash.

SOFT OPENING

I woke before you,

Hovered above
Your mouth a moment

As you lava-lamped
Under the sheets,
Our apartment a windsock

Limp as all elsewhere,
Quiet as the airspace

Above Pompeii.

THE BOMB

The beautiful bombs
In the dresses
On the dance floor
Are the sort of bombs

Worth going to war for.
Manley puffs out his chest,
Oppenheimer's khakis show
Signs of civil unrest.

They have mankind on the mind.
It's a bird, it's a plane,
It's a shame
Bombs are so bad at charades.

Big bombs are passé,
IEDs are all the rage.
A drone a day
Keeps the big bombs at bay.

I make my body
A bomb,
It's the best way
To get my chest off.

I'm your man,
I open up
At the bomb's behest,
In the flash of a lifespan.

EVERGLADES

Literally the richest bank in the world
Is twilight in a wilderness of error.
It does the opposite, a pride of lions.
I is the bearer of old news.
It is twilight lounging
On fronds of downtime.
I is the cabin laughing off the grid.
Your error wants inside,
Its mouth is frothing.
Twilight in a wilderness of error illuminates
Hooves holding the rifle of their offing.
I sense your conviction,
Sweetheart.
I object.

The richest bank in the world
Is a barber cutting hair in his own image.
His customers wear the opposite
Of a cape rising in the chair
To freshly sharpened hardware.
They stare into a mirror.
The mirrors inside stare back from behind.
A blonde boy sweeps the locks.
A neck bears the nick of a razor
And the barber bathes in the blood of another.
His apology can't be heard above his shears.
They have selective hearing.
Outside into a river of grass and mangrove
And *slam* and rain.

A lightning bolt came up to him.
He'd never seen anything so silver.
He notices the shop has Spanish moss.
The sightseers became curious
About the Miccosukee.
Along came souvenir shop owners
Insisting on gator wrestling.
If they had known fat cats killed curiosity
They never would have signed on the line.
Suddenly the shop is the gator hole of the soul.
The soul sways like Spanish moss.
They never say when
The dice are playing God again.
The Manatee Chief is retired.

The manatee wades out of the water and roars at the sightseers
That one of them owes him a drink.
From the beach below the boardwalk, *cock-a-doodle-do!*
What about a Christmas bowl cut over by the mangrove manatees!
Because in Florida there are Floridians
And they are born Floridians at large.
Every motion
Can't stop its own ocean.
The oceans' motions make mistakes.
Some of the dying are unspeakable
In their thinness, poorly disguised meat mannequins.
The mosquitoes are so big
They bleed you like a pig.
Being eaten alive is an acquired taste.

The last living breast man loses it and roars on the beach
That someone fucking owes him a fucking drink.
The surrounding bikinis all giggle.
This was the man who moved to amend the constitution
Once a week.
The manatee manhandled a heron
And ended up in captivity.
He became fluent in dolphin
And then became the breast man
Upon release. The manatee brought a knife fight to its knees
By giving a motivational dolphin speech.
Tears stood in the eyes of onlookers like lightning about to bolt
Toward the door of the storm.
Drowning out the deeps is the new norm.

Military personnel denounced the violent sea of green
Concealing inroads in full sunlight.
It is the inroads of the rascally American Indian
Made of powdered barber blood.
It is subtropical twilight the colour of Calusa
Hosting supernatural Spaniards
Above the white sands of the Keys.
They aim their solar panels.
It is black as a gator hole.
They intercept the airboat
And *I* is the first throat the gators taste.
The rifle of their offing is at the concierge.
It is twilight with a wilderness of error in the air.
Bang bang, silence sang.

The richest bank in the world shoots
Men into space from Kennedy in sponsored suits.
These narcoleptic stretches threaten the mission,
But work out with impunity in dreams.
The peninsula is problem-free,
Resolves its problems perfectly.
The breast men reassert themselves in red convertibles.
You are drunker than you think.
Some will not live to see tomorrow.
Others worship the real thing, asleep on the beach
In the spirit of scoring
On the empty net of heavenly bliss.
Chanel advises applying perfume where you want to be kissed.
I drown in fondue and good time.

Into the courtroom they go. *Into the courtroom they go.*
The boots on the ground are theirs. *The boots on the ground are theirs.*
The pride of lions lounges endlessly. *Cock-a-doodle-do!*
The bank lounges endlessly. *Cock-a-doodle-do!*
The barber withdrew his money from the town's hair, and boldly,
The blonde boy took a handsome cut. *Cock-a-doodle-do!* And there I was,
A lightning bolt at twilight in a wilderness of error.
The manatees and solar panels
Are the sightseers who wrestled the gators to death.
The dice are rolling out God's red carpet
Over a river of green that slithers out the door of the storm.
The boy is on a spending spree,
And I strike a deal
With our money's worth where my mouth is before the kitchen closes.

COURTESY CALL

Your mouth a gift shop,

As if a gift precedes its giving,

With boots on the ground

Of grounds for dismissal,

Missiles on course,

You phone to inform

Your mother

She is her own

Trojan Horse.

KING TIDE

The face of climate change has palm trees in its eyes.
Spoiler alert.
Everyone dies.

As sea levels rise the economy flounders,
The clouds are aroused.
They agree to a final mortgage cycle before the storm.

I invest my share of islandry.
Saying *yes* to an unknown is easy.
I have never really known my father

But I know his Miami house will have a hard time
Treading water.
Rising sea levels float my boat.

My father follows
The money.
Life is climate change.

While mammals in Miami double down,
Rising seas lift the spirits of every living thing
Below my boat.

I, alone, redefine the continental shelf.
I am the shit.
I'm full of myself.

INDEPENDENCE DAY

Strawberry jam, rhubarb chutney,
Chokecherry juice, bread and butters,
Basil beans, Mother's dill pickles.
Serviceberry jelly, spiced orange slices,
Rum raisins, okra, Delores's
Pickled prunes, chowchow, Connie's pear
Chutney, Robert's tea pickles, zydeco
Green beans, Louise's bread and butters,
Kosher dills, kumquat preserve,
Dried onions, corn, kale and chard,
Grannie's tongue pickles.
Korean turnips, Hungarian Hots,
Just-like-store-bought catsup,
Nancy Glover's tangerine butter,
Nebraska sweet dills, sun-dried tomatoes,
Celery in red miso, Mrs. Kim's pickled garlic,
Sophia's bread and butters,
Summer squash icebox pickles,
Martha Groeniger's chili sauce.
Rosehip jam, jalapeno-lime marmalade,
Overnight sunshine pickles,
Mary Randolph's sugar-free ketchup,
Sauerkraut with juniper berries,
Paradise jelly, paradise conserve,
Vietnamese bean sprouts, Jerusalem artichokes,
Lebanese eggplant, Polish mushrooms,
Lynda's dills, Win Way's dills, Sunchoke dills,
Priscilla Heindel's bread and butters,
Lillian Calhoun's apple-onion chutney,
Zucchini chips, Gladys's old-fashioned

Green tomato mincemeat with suet,
Pickled beef tongue, pig feet and ears,
Salmon, herring and oysters,
Taffy Strapp's beach plum jelly,
Madonna Joy Wilson's schleiss gurken,
Hope Alamo's buffaloberry jelly,
Salted duck eggs, crystal pickles, rat tails,
Solar glow honey spears,
Dehydrated sage, bread and butters *my* way,
Strawberries and stars,
Blushing angel, leather britches,
My apocalypse is going to be delicious.

SOLO SHOW

She calls it *All the Boys*
I'd Like to Fuck.
Ninety-nine
Young dreamboats

Rendered in ballpoint pen.
Then there's me.
There I am,
Number seventy-three,

Blurring the line
Between flower and weed.
Beauty is funny that way,
To each his own intone,

Depending on the day,
Like chandeliering ice.
She sells boys
Like toys at a boy store.

That's nice.
My self-esteem
Is beyond my control
Until I'm sold.

I'm feeling flirty
As a blossom on a stem.
I'm trying to turn thirty.
Like hell I am.

RAT'S ASS

I ran a relocation program
Spearheaded by the blade of a shovel.

Retired after one client.
Too involved.

Drove him into the driveway
A half-inch behind the ears.

A second or two of hind legs pedalling
And that was that.

Forget which hat I had on.
It's neither here nor there.

Same day Dad said, *Checked out a while ago.*
Kept mum. Best two cents I never spent.

Somewhere on Mars a rover passed.
The goats regurgitated red pasture grass.

THE MORNING AFTER

The field across from the telephone pole
I wrapped your car around
Is beautiful.
I cry

On the shoulder holding the steering wheel.
I come whenever I can feel my legs
And stand before the field that planted you.
The sky and horizon high-five

In the long run.
I feel bad for all of the backpacks in Boston,
Fondled by guards
Who presume no good.

This is the way it is.
This is the way it has to be
For me to wrap your car around
The middle of nowhere.

Poor planning is why
I'm among the survivors.
I raise my voice
As my own.

My heart goes out
To distracted drivers.
I have no choice.
All I hear is dial tone.

WATERLOO

You were a waist I fell in love with
When a waist was what I loved,
Living on King Street,
A blizzard of flesh in shining armour

Doubling down on my own advice,
Always an absence on hand,
Never tying the same knot twice.
Give a waist an inch and it takes a wife

To turn around eternity.
The eighties gave the gift of me,
Myself and lipo. I am the only family member
Who never had a tummy tuck.

I walked away
From a buffet of typos
And drove my cattle back to where
The battle over

The story of the battle began,
Rumours of the whole hog
Too good to screw.
Waterloo, my girl between girls,

My everything,
I love you,
You are what I eat.
I raise what I love for meat.

LIFE LESSONS

While I sleep,
A plane disappears over the Indian Ocean
Without a mayday call.
Without any mention of a misbehaving engine,

The radar simply loses sight,
The transponder falls asleep for the rest of its life
And the sun unveils the ballad of Big Deal.
A complete lack of debris

Keeps families in disbelief.
It rains everything in theory
The way real rain rains.
It rains *La Comédie humaine*,

Beads of blood in rosebud disguises
And drops of copyright joy I deploy
The way the Messiah rises.
It rains balls and chains from the ball and chain store,

Polonius pain, stewardess cries
And pilots galore.
It rains a plane like a model
Falling on a runway in the French Alps,

And the seatbelt light pings on.
I follow orders
And pray for the flight recorders
To the break of dawn.

HAPPY BELATED

Every morning you wake up dead,
The feeling of aliveness all in your head,
As if lingering pink feathers
From a bachelorette party the night before.
As if the deafening potential of white were good for nothing
But a dream ceasing behind closed doors.
As if light makes the dark darker.
As if evasive flowers,
A revenge fantasy of surviving the creator,
As if *The End* were inscribed on the inside of your eyelids,
You make the best of your emergency.
You might remember me from not showing up to parties.
It's too much fun
Staying home where the light shines on me
Like a rhinestone onesie.
Was there ever any question?
No wonder I'm dead, nobody said.

FALSE IDOL

The march against my father, who art alone,
Wandering the heavenly echelons of the food chain,
Whose will be done unto plot upon field of fiction
In the name of abundance, unknown known be thy name.
He whose skyscrapers rose to the occasion
Of snakes and ladders, brass ring rashes and gold holed up in silver mines.
He whose boss is a dick hungers to be in pole position.
He who made a first name for himself with the Lord in mind,
Pithy and civil, knowing it takes one feeling farmer to know another

And commodify the countryside.
Here was a man who never found out
What the third fork was for, whether love was the eleventh province.
He who reads after burning, knows what you need to know,
Who was and is and is to come, whose appearance would be his vanishing,
An invitation to an art opening thousands of years ago.
He who is unwelcome in his own Edenic dream
Of a nuclear family. Redemption is a hell of a thing,
Though they rarely roll the tape that far.

The march against the march against those with absent fathers
Shall inherit the earth, the birds in faulty feathers, the Father, the Ghost,
And the You within You, the saving lie of three being better than two.
In the name of all the time before you were born, and all the time
After you die, let beer bottles sweat before firepits
Like Christmas in July. Life's too long to edit. It's never too late
To become what you already are. Here is what you need to know.
All will be forgiven. What doesn't kill me disappoints me.
For the love of God, go to reception and ask for Andy.

SPRING

Time I slip
On that dress.
Time my closet
Tries cleanliness.
Time I whisper
It's time again
To every trampoline
On the block.
Cockeyed bunnies
Chop chop,
Flowers *oink*,
It pours
Pencil shavings
As if God
Were making
A point.

PONY BOY

You *swallowed* the key to my heart?
Bad pony. Hiding the oldest trick
In plain sight is the worst

Idea for a book. Your asshole
Is always the first place I look.
I wrote the book on the oldest trick,

I wrote it in invisible ink.
This Magic Eye stinks,
Everyone sees the dolphins but me.

The art at the Whitney
Really makes you think. *Security!*
I'm not smart enough for my own good.

My pony is proof.
It's all rabbits and hats
Until the moment of *poof.*

URN

We could all fly
Round trip to Greece
Ten thousand times
With the unredeemed
Frequent flyer miles
Of the deceased.

PLEASURE PRINCIPLE

Dallas is nice this time of year.
I hate it here, Debbie cheers.
She lives in Silicon Valley now
With a husband, two sons

And a past she plays down.
If it feels good, say it
With an air banner.
Take your fake fun and wax its wings

Until the sun comes home.
Has anyone seen my manners?
I open my mouth and these chickadees fly out.
My inner middle child fancies

A lifetime supply of Girls Gone Wild.
Christmas trees are native in the state I was raised.
Ask not what a dollar can do for you.
You can do a lot of living on minimum wage.

Only the sincere gain weight.
All passions,
Even unpleasant ones,
Stare down the barrel of heaven.

Wear your cake
Like a virtue.
Look with your eyes.
Nice guys finish after you.

WAITING ROOM

You never hear sirens at the hospital.

Just children wanting wheelchair rides,
The preface of high heels on tile.

Into the system he goes.

Where he stops, video evidence shows.

The security guard waits at his desk

For his first post-diploma test,
But the peace keeps itself in a room with TV.

Everyone chips a tooth on the books

And waits patiently.

He will never know the wards of rival surgeons.

The cafeteria line shuffles forward,

The disappointment of mashed potatoes palpable.

                    Justice is served

Without gravy,

A lucky lady or living will.

A nurse wakes him to take his sleeping pill.

GRAND BEND

Whatever I had
A hand in
Has become the brunt of
A rape joke.

You are what
You abandon.
When push comes to shove
You choke

And go down on your luck.
I make fail porn.
The critical masses
Can swallow my pride.

Wake up
And smell the chloroform,
You are not
Who I say you are.

The silver lining of
Your gold mine
Is sleep.
I know all too well

The rope
At the end of the rope
Is your only hope
In hell.

CONTRASTIVE FOCUS DUPLICATION

Grannie loved Grandpa
On my mother's side,
Like, *loved*-loved.

She believes he's above
With Aunt Margaret,
Who fell in the tub.

It was tragic, *tragic*-tragic.

Thirty years later, in Kenya,
Two trucks, head-on, one
Failing to contain my cousin.

Nora flew home
In a glorified Rubbermaid container.

Grannie remains
By the mouth of bone bridges,
Ready to *go*-go.

BUTCHERS HOLLER

On this street the lives are final drafts,
The protagonists are flags
And dogs walking owners bearing little bags.
The butter cuts beautifully for February.

My living situation is temporary,
I soak it up, a diligent sponge,
Asleep in the afternoon heat.
You know what they say, *do what you love*

And never live a day of your life.
There's plenty of fish in the barrel.
I'm a cherub in Estero,
Man-meat for the ladies' league,

A hunk the husbands despise.
Oh, relax, old man, take a look at my book,
I'm a lot like you. I never leave home without my hair,
I applaud your pride, coming to life

Like Hollywood Hogan, care of Viagra,
In star-spangled explosions.
Mothers cover their children's ears
As far away as Playa Negra.

Snug in the suburbs of the spirit,
Where the deer and the antelope pray,
Birthplace of the gold chain
Nestled in the chest hair of an open collar,

Freedom is measured in football fields,
God is a secret shopper,
The appeal of immaculate grass never grows old,
Heaven is a glorious ass with no hole.

I am giving myself the day off to turn thirty-two. I will be here, trying not to sound like an impersonator of what I think the world wants to hear. Nine times out of ten when I say *the world* I mean myself and probably am just about to have a beer on the porch and wait for a sudden gust of wind to lift a skirt. Thanks to whomever I thank for this, streets crawling with people whose hearts may soon be broken. I am suspicious of the city like I am the man whistling in a crowded locker room. At least one in five times when I say *suspicious* I mean *jealous*.

Once a year I remember I was born, momentarily the youngest person in the world like everyone else, my chances of someday being the oldest next to nothing like everyone else. Writing about childhood is boring and impossible, anyway. A period piece that keeps you from pointing your camera outside since every shot requires a Trans Am, Jordaches, shoulder pads and perms. I struggle to stay on budget as is. My life has been a succession of places I managed to stay broke, the piss and coffee of Parkdale the latest friends of the road to no riches. They used to call this the future.

One of the great solaces in life is that hundreds of years from now someone will apply prescription cream to a mysterious rash and perhaps read these words and find comfort in the fact that some things really do never change. Everyone watches helplessly as their generation runs mediocrity up the flagpole, prey to some new beast of convenience. *History remembers only the best of the worst ideas.* I have these words I wrote posted above my desk because I need to remind myself to do my *best* worst.

Your body is the only second language that let me learn it. I am sick to my stomach and overjoyed. I want to live everywhere, an architect afloat an ocean of feeling in a world where earthquakes are blamed for all the people buildings kill, and the change

I want to see is changing constantly in small and daily ways. Having tattoos means I never have to wonder if I should get one. This seems to me sound logic for having kids. I have found the biggest questions in life evaporate in the affirmative, which may sound like the most obvious thing, but when it comes to wisdom not many think to look on the bottoms of their shoes, in the cotton balls of fresh pill bottles or the simple elegance of a cheese pizza.

Honesty is the oldest trick in the book, and it occurs to me that maybe not every moment is meant to be experienced with the enthusiasm of a cover band on the fall fair circuit. Not all trouble needs to end with *I love you*. Eleven thousand days on Earth have taught me that some jerk will always take the middle urinal. Never engage the bullshit machine, or for that matter go to bed dead. When I said I was suspicious of the city I meant suspicious of the world, and by *the world* I mean myself, my own contribution to the bullshit.

I have given up on getting a blurb. *Blurbs are where you hear writers you respect sounding like utter fools*, a writer I respect once told me. That might be the best blurb ever, but respectability talks one out of even the best of a bad thing such as blurbs, the lower back tattoos of literature.

If you Google *johnny paycheck corpse* the last image in the search is a sand sculpture of a giant dragon emerging from the beach and swallowing a sand sculptor made of sand. I am telling you because this may not be the case tomorrow. I am a secessionist in this city, miming my symptoms, a hitch searching for a horse. Nothing can be done. I simply have to let it pass through my system, this benign mass on the imagination the world couldn't care less about. When I go back to work, *I am disappearing* are the first words out of my mouth.

MASK CLASS

An actress meets a man playing her partner
And sparks fly.
She wants the shipwreck of his prior life
Off her rocks pronto.

He has a hazmat team clean up.
Every last dandelion must go.
The two are completely herbicidal.
He buys her a best friend forever and she feels bridal.

Second marriages come first.
You figure out what to do and what not to
And smile for the camera
And your character comes true

When someone slaps you on Seventh Avenue
For that thing you did in the last episode.
They play a man and woman
Walking down Seventh Avenue

Holding hands with the spark that got them the job.
They love to forget.
They live for the future alone
And tell themselves,

There was only ever you,
When love is actually a bitch
With more bones than it knows
What to do with.

ISLAND TIME

A tropical day above the law
Is a fine place to get your mail.
I have zero reservations
About taking to the heartland
With a crosscut saw.
Outside the jurisdiction of progress bars,
I occupy the pulpit
Of two minds, a student of rooftops, the joy
Of abandon and deathbed conversions,
The ghost in the meat machine
That keeps my stardust skeleton warm.
I am a heavy sleeper.
I reach rock bottom and dig deeper,
Absent without leave and loving
The broken yolk of every minute since we met,
A regular astride his usual stool.
A reason to wake is worth its weight
In greater grails. Wanting it both ways
Is the one true path.
You have to go for me to miss you.
You do the math.
I saw the future in a photograph of a sunset
And suddenly knew
I want to do all of my losing with you.

FOREVERMARK

I feel alive inside the story of my life
Is the story I gave the border guard.
Forever is a long story.
This line is taking forever.

A line attracts too much attention
To hire a second bartender.
I gave forever to a woman once.
Jesus will be back before she is.

Everything forever needs to not be here is.
Everything is something else.
This line is something else.
Diamonds dancing on a glass floor

Show birthday balloons what floors are for.
The birthday boy collapses and his diamond yells for help.
Forever never ends well.
The man turns blue as they wheel him away.

Dancing resumes after forever ties its shoe,
Diamonds swallowing the spot
Where every now and then
A mountain on the move starts pulling out all the stops.

WORST CASE SCENARIO

Nude at a nude beach, the worst case scenario happens.
I walk around with my worst case scenario
As if nothing is wrong. Nothing *is* wrong.
A worst case scenario is only natural.

I notice others,
Some delight in our passing.
My worst case scenario is basking in afternoon sun
And everyone is fine.

This is my idea of a good time!
There's nothing worse than a worst case scenario
Outstaying its welcome and starting to hurt.
Like lemon juice on a wound

My worst case scenario squirts,
Blood slowly flows back upon my brain
And the worst is yet to come
Once again.

YULETIDE

Oh, the weather outside is weather,
And worshippers look more and more
Like leather as they lie
Under the burning bindi of our solar system.

I wake up this way,
Twenty minutes north of Naples,
And empty my stocking of eye candy.
All Estero wants for Christmas is incorporation

And enough foreign workers for tillage.
It takes a newly anointed village
To raise a little oblivion.
This year they started naming winter storms.

On Atlas, on Boreas, on Cleon, on Dion!
On Electra, on Falco,
On Gemini, Hercules and Ion!
Watching the Weather Channel

Reminds me of Ontario fields
Learning how to sleep for the umpteenth time
While coyotes come and go
Like the picaresque heroes they are.

When we talk about palm trees
We talk about ordering Jeff's Chinese on Boxing Day.
We talk about Kronos, Leon, Maximus, Nika, benign
In the image of a radar

And how a long succession of days
In the high twenties
Can make you think you love someone
More than you actually do.

We drive an hour north
To Casey Key to be
With friends for New Year's Eve.
Onto the island we go.

The subtropics draw closer
As we crawl down the narrow road,
Past the estate of Stephen King,
And I think, *Really, Steve?*

A mall cop in a custom Corolla?
His house is out of sight.
Forty-acre buffers make good neighbours.
The day is darker,

The palm blades sharper in yards
Where shadows kick back in the shade,
Fifty feet from the shore.
We swim with a school of stingrays

In the sequined morning sun
As it glitters on the surface
Of day one
Of a new year.

You don't have to be a strong swimmer
When each day comes with a celery-salt rimmer
And trouble is harder to find
Than a love like mine.

On Orion, on Pax, on Quintus, on Rex!
On Seneca and Titan,
On Ulysses and Vulcan!
Coyote adapts to the shores of the Gulf

Where the American pulse
Runs out of steam
And the end of America
Forgets what it means

And seniors suffer
Strokes every hour,
And dolphins are
The number-one stocking stuffer.

On Wiley, on Xenia, on Yona, on Zephyr!
Onward, my gold mine!
Onward, having never been better!
When it comes to the tip of Florida,

All the time in the world
Is ending all the time.
You can almost hear the smiles
Going down.

ART BASEL

All is nothing.
If the world were fair
There would be no rollercoasters.
Fuck fair.

Fuck feeling.
Fuck what you know.
Fuck fairness and feeling
Is my new motto.

Knowing who's who
Is all in the shoes.
You should also know the work
On the wall gave its all

And all it got was a man
Swanning across a Miami floor
With rollercoaster hair.
He might have freshened up.

He could give a flying fuck.
All is nothing more
Than Ontario
All winter long,

When all song stops.
The man will never know.
The swan is not all there.
The world is not fair.

THE LONG FETCH

Under a fluorescent Amazon sky
A slave places orders
On a conveyor belt.
A screen spells out each step
Clear as a crystal skull,
Threatening to beat his eardrums to dust

In the open air of the warehouse.
Ear protection is a must.
An online petition to save the slave circulates.
You think you can help?
You flatter yourself.
The CEO makes a statement under duress

And purchases eight hundred acres of rainforest.
What happens online leaves others behind.
I couldn't care less
What happens offline.
Nature fakes its way across the rainforest floor
In a marvellous feat of modern technology.

The mind behind the warehouse design
Has nature down to a T.
A beautiful mind always has haters,
Slaves to the drumbeat of change.
They think they can help.
They flatter themselves.

Under the fluorescents the flock looks almost artful
Faking its way along the campaign trail.
I am no help.
I master myself
And check out
And qualify for free shipping.

On a screen I monitor my order
In real time.
The slaves are shipped from Tripoli,
Shoulder to shoulder on deck,
Surrounded by nothing but Mediterranean for days.
The man next to me falls, ironically,

To the floor of the world's largest floating pharmacy.
A pregnant woman begins to scream and vomit.
Someone shouts from a lower level,
I'm having a hard time breathing!
And receives a complimentary beating
With nowhere to go but what looks like ocean.

The captain keeps his options open.
Just when you think you smell olives,
He and his crew abandon ship
And the unmanned liner lurches onward,
The living dream of refugees
Woken by the toe of Italy.

PACIFIC GESTURE

Your roundabout reasons why

You regifted yourself to the sea

Slid through my mail slot nonchalantly,

Sealed in a manila love tunnel,

Like a hydro wire wearing

One too many birds for a Monday.

SHOTGUN INFINITY

These days the hours look after
Are a single sentence I revise.
They give birth on a treadmill
And practice beheading.
Talk about silence.

I hate sitting still.
I do.
I lap dance myself outside
And make do with less than everything,
Less than I should, and so should you.

God is good,
God is green,
Bless this boulder of fatherly love
I was born beneath.
These days the hours look after abandon lifeboats left and right.

I paint bowls of light bulbs
As South Florida continues to prove more Florida than Florida,
Hawking shades of orange at golden hour
Some will never see.
God yodels *Allahu Akbar* with alarming regularity and flees

From the last bridge burning with glee.
The government gets a green light to level every mountain and tree
So they can see Him coming.
They monitor every man
With a beard that seems to say, *You're not the boss of me.*

Things are not as they kick and scream to be.
They are just like you and me.
We fail to touch much.
These days the hours look after my soft spot
For the smell of rain.

They put car after car on the road
In the land of death chants, breakdowns and tropical injustice.
Pain is in the limousine.
The waiter knows what I mean
When I complain about the swan in my swan

And drinks are on the house.
We waste our breath,
The only question is when.
The swan moves on
In one of my moods

And makes do with too much beauty
And so should you.
These days the hours look after rock
With a shotgun on a Panhandle porch
On an afternoon scorcher

And the minutes drip seconds like Chinese water torture.
One way and another,
I forget how to leave the house
And communicate only with my eyebrows.
The last thing I vacuum is always my feet

Like a good totalitarian.
I fall asleep and dream in American
Because the country club has no book,
Because a hook to hang my goodness has no book,
Because breaking a band of wild horses

Is the first thing I think of when I think about waking.
These days the hours look after enclose
Photos of flowers and birds for those
Without a garden.
You forget how it feels

To turn thirteen, the smell of snow,
And the time between washing your hands
And starting to touch the world again.
Across from the most shelled hotel in history,
A boy holds a balloon.

I watch from the lobby as he lets it go.
Helium does its thing.
The heroes of tomorrow tend to the fallen
Like there's no tomorrow.
I sing like so.

Nothing happened that year.
No one was born, no one moved away,
The days conflated like a Florida winter,
The smallest gestures exploding

In the Saharan sprawl of every hour.
You did nothing for the houseplants
Except keep them alive, ate next to nothing,
Dug heels deep into weeks without speaking

Until Elvis broke character outside
The Legion. People were pissed.
You cried yourself to sleep for something to do.
The morning after the morning after

The new you was nothing like you imagined.
Nothing may be irrelevant. When they ask,
You saw nothing. Nothing is the elephant
In the room, not even the elephant.

TAIL

As long as love is odourless,
Noses are useless.
As long as rubble enlists a loader,
Putting boulders to bed remains
Foremost for the foreman.
As long as porn runs errands for Eros,
Ruins relocate to the place
Where all the waterbeds went.
The land of headstones with strange inscriptions
Is a coffee table book waiting to happen.
As long as speech bubbles of February breath
Require serious effort, and all that sleeps
Under the snow of unfinished business
Wades the swamps of the unconscious, some
Will pretend to not know what water is.
As long as the calendars of celebrity chefs
Await dinner invitations, onions continue
To sway elections in India. The last letters of the alphabet
Deter the uninitiated. Bus drivers tell the best stories
And Buddy McKenzie dons his crown
Of pork rinds for a fourteen-hour cigarette
Across the Midwest. As long as the politics of circles
Leave us alone, married to mystery, we wipe
Small spills up with our socks, find late-life
Comfort in the valleys of spoons, farm *For Sale*
Signs for sale, houses benign as abandoned
Beehives full of flies, the all-time unforgettable
Breasts of cinema and the concluding minutes of hours,
As loose ends on TV meet their maker
And fakers find God in certified silence.
As long as those who feel like cymbal solos

Most mornings forget the face they first made
Upon finding the world can be a shitty place,
Librarians tap the shoulders of those whose
Headphone frequencies are causing complaints.
As long as our wildest dreams take walks
After dinner, metal detectors scour seas
Of treasure trails, the living mist of memory, pressing for
A world where the price of living like gods is not shame,
A recollection of warmth in the middle of winter,
The possibility of dignity in bowling shoes,
Spreading outward like the jams of forbidden fruit, thinking
I want to tell you something,
I feel I want to tell you something,
Something that swallows its own end and gags,
How all's well when it wags.

ONE TOO MANY

The pool after hours asks not for forgiveness.
The sky dark and sparkly
Two hundred miles above us,
Another government satellite assumes its place in space,
Blushes at the sight of our poolside suits

And logs our infrared figures.
On nights like tonight the middle can suddenly
Go on sale without a hatch to batten
When all of the trees I've ever mistreated begin converging
On my cabin.

That was quite the party,
I must say.
The pool after hours normally sorts itself out,
But Syria has become a bacteria,
A playground for grown men with Kalashnikovs.

I shoot my mouth off
Because fun will always find funding.
Having fun is infectious.
Tip one bellboy well and business booms.
You have to be a little human

To slip past security for a midnight dip.
I whisper to your thighs and word spreads
Under dark and sparkly skies.
The pool after hours is all ears.
The satellite starts singing

The heart of its hard drives out.
It tells the bellboy what to bring.
A good long game can survive the pink part of anything.
I stop making sense
And every single thing I know

For a moment smells like pool.
As we polish off the Pinot,
A satellite of lust acquires life on earth.
There is no God.
There are no words.

ABOUT THE AUTHOR

Andy McGuire is from Grand Bend, Ontario, and currently resides in Toronto. He is pursuing an MFA in creative writing from the University of Guelph. McGuire's poems have appeared in *Riddle Fence*, Hazlitt, *The Walrus* and *Eleven Eleven*. His website is www.andymcguire.ca.

ACKNOWLEDGEMENTS

Grateful acknowledgement is made to the editors of the following publications, in which some of these poems appeared in earlier drafts: *Riddle Fence*, Hazlitt, *The Walrus* and *Eleven Eleven*.

I am also grateful for the support of the Ontario Arts Council.

Thanks to Karen Schindler, Karen Solie, Kevin Connolly, Alana Wilcox, everyone at Coach House Books, Kim Dorland, Jeramy Dodds and Shauna Born.

Typeset in Oneleigh (cover) and Laurentian (text). Laurentian was designed by Rod McDonald in 2003 for *Maclean's* magazine – the first text typeface ever commissioned by a Canadian magazine. Its design took reference of the types designed by Claude Garamond and William Caslon. McDonald blended these two influences together and gave his alphabet a strong vertical stress, high x-height and narrow proportions to allow the font to function well in tight settings.

Printed at the old Coach House on bpNichol Lane in Toronto, Ontario, on Zephyr Antique Laid paper, which was manufactured, acid-free, in Saint-Jérôme, Quebec, from second-growth forests. This book was printed with vegetable-based ink on a 1965 Heidelberg KORD offset litho press. Its pages were folded on a Baumfolder, gathered by hand, bound on a Sulby Auto-Minabinda and trimmed on a Polar single-knife cutter.

Edited by Jeramy Dodds
Designed by Heidi Waechtler
Cover image: Detail from *Midnight* by Kim Dorland, 2010. Oil, acrylic and gems on linen, 42 × 72 inches. Courtesy of the artist.
Author photo by Shauna Born

Coach House Books
80 bpNichol Lane
Toronto ON M5S 3J4
Canada

416 979 2217
800 367 6360

mail@chbooks.com
www.chbooks.com